The Wandering Host

Fourth Source Explorations

Matrika Press is proud to publish this manuscript of David Starr Jordan.

It has been edited and arranged by "Twinkle" Marie Manning and published by Matrika Press according to the public domain copyright laws and with intent of ensuring such important spiritual works remain in print and available for future generations to access.

The Wandering Host

David Starr Jordan

Edited and arranged by:
"Twinkle" Marie Manning

Matrika Press
Publisher

Arrangement Copyright © Marie Manning

September 2016

All Rights Reserved
including the right of reproduction,
copying, or storage in any form
or means, including electronic,
In Whole or Part,
without prior written
permission of the author

ISBN: 978-1-946088-02-4

Library of Congress Control Number: 2016917091
1.Spiritual Exploration 2.Christian 3.Unitarian Universalism 4.Title

Matrika Press
164 Lancey Street
Pittsfield, Maine
(760) 889-5428
Editor@MatrikaPress.com

Matrika Press

www.MatrikaPress.com

Original Content Copyright by David Starr Jordan circa 1904
Printed in the USA

"When man shall rise to manhood's destiny,
When our slow-toddling race shall be full grown,
Deep in each human heart a chamber lone
Of holies, holiest shall builded be,
And each man for himself must hold the key.
Each man must kindle his own altar fires,
Each burn an offering of his own desires,
And each, at last, his own High Priest shall be!"

~ David Starr Jordan

Author's Dedication

To my Wife
Jessie Knight Jordan

Editor's Dedication

For the voices throughout history in the hope they shall remain intact and ever positively influence future generations.

For Jo, because she adores Jesus!

And, for Jason, just because...

The Wandering Host

Fourth Source Explorations

Publisher's Note

Two of our focuses at Matrika Press are to preserve texts and thoughts of our ancestors, and to create publications that share the values and principles of Unitarian Universalism. This allegorical story by David Starr Jordan is a tale about the search for spiritual meaning. Symbolic of Jesus Christ's ministry, it succinctly embodies our Christian heritage and the fourth of the six sources we draw our faith from, namely that which calls us to respond to God's love by loving our neighbors as ourselves.

This manuscript was initially printed under the title of "The Story of the Innumerable Company" by Messrs. Whitaker & Ray, of San Francisco. Later, with edits by the author, published in 1904 by the The University Press, Cambridge, U.S.A.

David Starr Jordan was the first President of Stanford University, and also the President of Indiana University. He was a pacifist and ichthyologist.

While he never officially became either a Unitarian or Universalist, he held liberal religious beliefs, and was said to be a regular philosophical spokesperson of the American

Unitarian Association.

He reputedly chose Starr for his middle name because of his love for astronomy and to honor his mother's respect for the Unitarian minister, Thomas Starr King.

As the story goes, his parents had been Baptists when they first married, but turned away from that religion *"because of their doubts as to 'eternal damnation.'"* They became Universalists and thus raised David without religious orthodoxy and rather within the framework of a living tradition that would evolve into Unitarian Universalism.

David Starr Jordan's manuscript has been edited by "Twinkle" Marie Manning and it is with humble privilege we resurrect this piece of our literary history.

We publish this work in deep gratitude to the online archives and other resources that house manuscripts to source and attribute ancient and otherwise lost works that are in the Public Domain. We encourage readers to support the ongoing existence and maintenance of the Public Domain archives and the publishing of such works.

For more information, visit:

http://matrikapress.com/publicdomainworks

- Matrika Press Independent Publisher

Fourth Source Explorations

The Wandering Host

There was once a great mountain which rose from the shore of the sea, and on its flanks it bore a mighty forest. The slopes of the mountain were green with soft grass and white and rosy with the flowers of spring. But beyond the crest the mountain grew harsh and wild, then ridges and gullies, peaks and chasms, springs and torrents. Farther on lay a sandy desert, which stretched its monotonous breadth to the shore of a wide, swift river. What lay beyond the river no one knew, because its shores were always hid in azure mist.

The Wandering Host

Year by year there came up from the shore of the sea an innumerable company of men and women. Each one must hasten over the green meadows to cross the mountain and the forest, faring onward toward the desert and the river. And this was one condition of the journey, that whosoever came to the river must breast its waters alone. Why this was so, no one could tell; nor did any one know aught of the land beyond. For of the multitude who had crossed the river not one had ever returned.

Fourth Source Explorations

As time went on, there came to be paths through the forest. Through its meadows no one seemed to need a path, but on the mountain to go without a guide seemed hopeless. Those who went first left traces to serve as guides for those coming after. Some put marks on the trees; some built little cairns of stones to show the way they had taken in going around great rocks. Those who followed found these marks and added to them. And many of the travelers left little charts which showed where the cliffs and chasms were, and by what means one could reach the hidden springs.

So in time it came to pass that there was scarcely a tree on the mountain which bore not some traveller's mark; there was scarcely a rock that had not a cairn of stones upon it. In early times there was One who came up from the sea and made the journey over the mountain and across the desert by a way so fair that the memory of it became a part of the story of the forest.

The Wandering Host

Men spoke to one another of his way, and many wished to find it out, that haply they might walk therein. He, too, had left a Chart, which those who followed him had carefully kept, and from which they had drawn help in many times of need.

The way he went was not the shortest way, nor was it the easiest. The ways that are short and easy lead not over the mountain. But his was the most repaying way. It led by the noblest trees, the fairest outlooks, the sweetest springs, the greenest pastures, and the shadow of great rocks in the desert.

It was as if the breath of the fresh blooming meadows followed one all the way through the forest. And the chart of his way which he left was very simple and very plain,-- easy to understand. Even a child might use it. And indeed there were many children who did so.

Fourth Source Explorations

On this chart were the chief landmarks of the region, the mountain with its forest, the desert with its green oases, the flower-carpeted pastures of the high lands, the paths to the hidden springs. But there were not many details. The old cairns were not marked upon it; and when two paths led alike over the mountain, there was no sign to show that one was to be taken rather than the other. Not much was said as to what food one should take, or what raiment one should wear, or by what means one should defend himself. But there were many simple directions as to how one should act on the road, and by what signs he should know the right path.

The Wandering Host

One ought to look upward, and not downward; to look forward, and not backward; to be always ready to give a helping hand to his neighbor: and whomsoever one meets is one's neighbor, he said.

Fourth Source Explorations

As to the desert, one need not dread it; nor should one fear the river, for the lands beyond it were sweet and fair. Moreover, one should learn to know the forest, that he might choose his course wisely. And this knowledge each one should seek for himself.
For, as he said, *"If the blind lead the blind, both shall fall into the ditch."*

The Wandering Host

There were many who followed his way and gave heed to his precepts. The path seemed dangerous at times, especially at the outset; for it lay along dizzy heights, through tangled underwood, and across swollen torrents. But after a while all these were left behind.

The way passed on between cleft rocks, into green pastures, and by still waters; and in the desert were sweet springs which gave forth abundantly, and about each spring the flowers sprang up fast in their season.

But some who tried to follow him said that his Chart was not explicit enough. Each step in the journey, they contended, should be laid out exactly; for to travel safely one should never be left in doubt.

Fourth Source Explorations

Now, it chanced that on the slope of the mountain there was a huge granite rock, which stood in the midst of the way. Some of the travelers passed to the right of it, while others turned to the left. Strangely enough, the Chart said nothing concerning this rock. No hint was given as to how one should pass by it.

The Wandering Host

When they came to the rock, many of the travelers took counsel one of another, and at last a great multitude was gathered there. Which way had he taken? For in the path he took they must surely go.

Many scanned the rock on every side, to find if haply he had left some secret mark upon it. But they found none; or, rather, no one could convince the others that the hidden marks he found were intended for their guidance.

Fourth Source Explorations

At nightfall, after much discussion, the old men in the council gave their decision. The safe way led to the right.

So he who kept the Chart marked upon it the place of the rock, and he wrote upon the Chart that the one true path leads to the right.

Henceforth each man should know the way he must go.

Moreover, those who bore the records showed that this decision was justified.

They wrote upon the Chart a long argument, chain upon chain and reason upon reason, to prove that from the beginning it was decreed that this rock be the test of the destiny of every man.

The Wandering Host

But in spite of argument, there were still some who chose the left-hand path because they verily believed that this was the only right way.

They, too, justified their course by arguments, line upon line and precept upon precept. And each band tried to make its following as large as it could.

Some men stood all day by the side of the rock, urging people to come with them to the right or to the left.

For, strangely enough, although each man had his own journey to make, and must cross the river at last alone, he was eager that all others should go along with him.

Fourth Source Explorations

And as each band grew larger, its members took pride in the growth of its numbers. In the larger bands, trumpets were blown, harps were sounded, and banners were waved in the wind.

Those who walked shoulder to shoulder under waving flags, to the sound of trumpets, felt secure and confident, while those who journeyed alone seemed always to walk with fear and trembling.

It was said in the old Chart that where two or three were gathered together on the way, strength and courage would be given them.

But men could not believe this, and few had the heart to test whether it were true or no.

So the bands went on to the right or to the left, each in its chosen path.

The Wandering Host

But after they had passed the first great rock, they came to other rocks and trees and places of doubt. Other councils were held, and at each step there were some who would not abide by the decision of the elders.

So these from time to time went their own ways. And they made new inscriptions on the Chart, and erased the old ones, each according to his own ideas.

And there was much pushing and jostling when the bands separated themselves one from another.

At last one of the oldest travellers in the largest band--a man with a long white beard, and wise with the experience of years--arose and said that not in anger, nor in strife, should they journey on.

Fourth Source Explorations

Discord and contention arise from difference of opinion. Let all men but think alike, and they will walk in peace and harmony. Let each band choose a leader. Let him carry the Chart, and let him night and day pore over its precepts. No one else need distress himself. One had only to keep step on the road, and to follow wherever the leader might direct.

The Wandering Host

So the people chose a leader, a man grave and serious, wise in the lore of the forest and the desert. He noted on the Chart each rock and tree, drawing in sharp outlines every detail in the only safe path. Moreover, all deviating trails he marked with the symbol of danger.

Fourth Source Explorations

And it came to pass that day by day other bands followed, and to them the Chart was given as he had left it. And these bands, too, chose leaders, whose part it was to interpret the Chart. But each one of these added to the Chart some better way of his own, some short cut he had found, or some new trail not marked with the proper sign of warning.

And with all these changes and additions, as time went on, the true way became very hard to find. At one point, so the story is told, there were twenty-nine distinct paths, leading in as many directions; each of these, if the Chart be true, came to its end in some frightful chasm.

With these there was a single narrow trail that led to safety; but no two leaders could agree as to which was the right trail. One thing only was certain: the true way was very hard to find, and no traveller might discover it unaided.

And some declared that the Chart was complicated beyond all need.

There was one who said, *"The multiplication of non-essentials has become the bane of the forest."*

Even a little meadow which he had found, and which he called the *"Saints' Rest,"* was so entangled in paths and counter-paths that, once out of sight of it, one could never find it again.

Fourth Source Explorations

All this time there were many bands that wandered about in circles, finding everywhere cairns of stones, but no way of escape.

Still others remained day after day in the shadow of great rocks, disputing and doubting as to how they should pass by them. There were arguments and precedents enough for any course; but arguments and precedents made no man sure.

And it came to pass that most travellers, followed the band they found nearest. At last, to join some band became their only care; and they looked with pity and distrust upon those who travelled alone.

The Wandering Host

But the bands all made their way very slowly.

No matter how wise the leader, not all were ready to move at once, and not all could keep step to the sound of even the slowest trumpet.

There was often much ado at nightfall over the pitching of the tents, and many were crowded out into the forest.

At times also, in the presence of danger, fear spread through the band, and many of the weaker ones were trampled on and sorely hurt.

Then, too, as they passed through the rocky defiles, some of them lost sight of the banners, and then the others would wait for them, or perchance leave them behind, to struggle on as best they might without chart or guide.

Fourth Source Explorations

And there were those who spoke in this wise way:
"Many paths lead over the mountain, and sooner or later all come to the desert and the river. It does not matter where we walk; the question is, How? We cannot know step by step the way he went. Let us walk by faith, as he walked. If our spirit is like his, we shall not lack for guidance when we come to the crossing of the ways."

And so they fared on. But many doubted their own promptings. *"Tell me, am I right?"* each one asked of his neighbor; and his neighbor asked it again of him.

And those who were in doubt followed those who were sure.

The Wandering Host

So it came to pass that these who walked by faith likewise gathered themselves into great companies, and each company followed some leader. Some of these leaders had the gift of woodcraft, and saw clearly into the very nature of things.

But some were only headstrong, and these proved to be but blind leaders of the blind.

Then one said, "*We must not be filled with our own conceit, but must humbly imitate him. We must try to work as he worked; to rest as he rested; to sleep as he slept. The deeds we do should be those he did, and those only. For on his Chart he has told us, not the way he went past rocks and trees, but the actions with which his days were filled.*"

Fourth Source Explorations

Then those who tried to do as he had done, moved by his motives and acting through his deeds, found the way wonderfully easy. The days and the hours seemed all too short for the joy with which they were filled.

But, again, there were many who said that his directions were not explicit enough. The Chart said so little. *"That we may make no mistake,"* they said, *"We must gather ourselves in bands and choose leaders. We cannot act as he acted unless there is some one to show us how."*

The Wandering Host

Thus it came to pass that leaders were chosen who could do everything that he had done, in all respects, according to his method.

And they added to the Chart the record of their own practices, not only that *"He did thus and so,"* but also, *"Thus and so he did not do." "Thus and thus did he eat bread, and thus only. Thus and thus did he loose his sandals. In this way only gave he bread and wine. Here on the way he fasted; there he feasted. At this turn of the road he looked upward thus, shading his eyes with his hand. Here he anointed his feet; there his face wore a sad smile. Such was the cut of his coat; of this wood was his staff; of such a number of words his prayer."*

And many were comforted in the thought that for every turn in the road there was some definite thing which he had done, and which they, too, might perform.

Fourth Source Explorations

Thus the duties of every moment were fixed.

But as the days went on these duties grew more and more difficult.

No one had time to look at the rocks or trees; no one could cast his eyes over a noble prospect; no one could stop to rest by the sweet fountains or in the refreshing shadows.

One could hardly give a moment to such things, lest he should overlook some needful service.

Then many lost heart, and said that surely he cared not for times and observances, else he would have said more about them.

When he made the journey, it was his chief reproach that he heeded not these things.

The Wandering Host

With him, ceremony or observance rose directly out of the need for it, each one as the need was felt. To imitate him is to feel as he felt.

With him feelings gave rise to word and action. *"So will it be with us. It is not for us to imitate him in the fashion of his coat or the cut of his beard. He went over the road giving help and comfort, as the sun gives light or the flowers shed fragrance, all unconscious of the good he did."*

And in this wise did many imitate him.

Fourth Source Explorations

They turned aside the boughs of the trees, that the sunshine of heaven might fall upon their neighbors.

And, behold, the same sunshine fell upon them also.

They removed the stones from the road, that others might not stumble over them; and others removed the stones from their way also.

The Wandering Host

But many were still in doubt and hesitation. The record, they said, was not explicit enough.

They counseled together, and gathered in bands, and chose leaders who should tell them how to feel. And the leaders gave close heed to all his feelings and to the times and seasons proper to each.

Here he was joyous, and at a signal all the band broke into merry laughter. Here he was stern, and the multitude set its teeth. There he wept, and tears fell like rain from innumerable eyes.

Fourth Source Explorations

As time went on, repeated action made action easy. The springs of feeling were readily troubled. Still each one felt, or tried to feel, all that he should have felt. No one dared admit to his fellows that his tears were a sham, his joy a pretense, his sadness a lie. But often, in the bottom of their hearts, men would confess with real tears that they had no genuine feeling there.

The Wandering Host

Then the people asked for leaders who could bring out real feelings. And there arose leaders, who by terrible words could fill the hearts with fear; by burning words could stir the embers of zeal; by the intensity of their own passions could fill the throng with pity, with sorrow, or with indignation. And the multitude hung on their lips; for they sought for feelings real and not simulated.

But here again division arose; for not all were touched alike by those who had power over the hearts of men. Some followed the leader who moved them to tears; others chose him who filled them with fear and trembling. Still others loved to linger in the dark shadow of remorse. Some said that right emotions were roused by loud and ringing tones. Some said that the tones should be sad and sweet.

Then there were some who said that feelings such as all these were idle and common.

When he trod the way of old, it was with radiant eyes and with uplifted heart. He saw through the veil of clouds to the glory which lay beyond.

We follow him best when we too are uplifted. Now and then on the way come to us moments of exultation, when we tread in his very footsteps.

These are the precious moments; then our way is his way. In the rosy mists of morning we may behold the glory which encompassed him.

The Wandering Host

In moments of silent communion in the forest we may feel his peace steal over us.

In the lilies of the field we find the perfection of his arrayment.

In the gentle rain that falls upon the just and the unjust we may know the soft pity of his tears.

When the sun declines, its last rays touch with gold the far-off mountain-tops beyond the great river.

Fourth Source Explorations

And the uplifting of great moments, filling the souls of men with peace that passeth understanding, came to many.

As they went their way, this peace fell upon their neighbors also. And no man did aught to make them afraid. And others sought to go with these, and thus they became a great band.

So they chose as their leaders those whose visions were brightest. And they made for themselves a banner like the white mist flung out from the mountaintops at the rising of the sun.

They spoke much to one another concerning the white banner and the peace which filled their souls.

The Wandering Host

But as they journeyed along, the dust of the way dimmed the banner, and the bright visions one by one faded away. At last they came no more.

Then the people murmured and called upon the leaders to grant them some brighter vision, something that all could see and feel at once: Some sign by which they might know that they were still in his way. *"Cause that a path be opened through the thicket,"* they said, *"and let a white dove come forth to lead us on; or let the mists beyond the river part for a moment, that we may behold the far country beyond."*

Fourth Source Explorations

And one of the leaders standing at the head of the column, clothed in the morning light as with a garment, raised his staff high in the air.

The sun's rays fell upon it, touching the morning mists with gold, and threw across them the long shadow of the upraised staff.

The shadow fell far out across the plains, and about it was a halo of bright light. And all the band looked joyfully at the vision.

Down the slope of the mountain and out into the plain they followed the way of the shadow.

And all the time the white banner waved at the head of the column.

The people said little to one another, but that little was a word of praise and rejoicing.

The Wandering Host

But it came to pass, as the day wore on, that the sun rose in the sky, and drew the mists up from the valley.

With them vanished the long shadow of the staff, and in its place appeared the sandy plain.

The feet of the people were sore with the rocks and stones. The air was thick with dust.

Their hearts were uplifted no longer. Instead they were filled with doubt and distress.

And the people repined and murmured against their leader.

Fourth Source Explorations

But the leader said that all was well; even in the way he went there had been stones and hindrances. More than once had he carried a heavy burden along a dusty road. But he never doubted nor complained, and so the radiance round about him never faded away.

But all the more the people clamored for a sign. *"Let the bright vision of the morning appear to us again."*

At length, worn with much entreaty, the leader raised once more his staff above his head. The sun at noon fell upon it.

But as the people gazed they saw no long line of radiance stretching out across the plains amid a halo of shining mist.

The shadow of the staff was a little shapeless mark upon the sand at their very feet.

The Wandering Host

Then the leader cast his staff away and went by himself alone, sad and sorrowful. That night, as he lay by the roadside, he looked upward to the clear, calm, honest stars.

They seemed to say to him, *"See all things as they really are. This was his way. 'In spirit and in truth' means in the light of no illusion. Not all the visions of mist or of sunshine can make the journey other than it is."*

Fourth Source Explorations

So he came to look closely at all things on the road.

Day by day he read the lessons of the desert and the mountain.

He learned to know directions by the growth of the trees.

By the perfume of the lilies he sought out the hidden springs.

By the red clouds at evening he knew that the sky would be fair.

By the red light in the morning he was warned of the coming storm.

And there were many who followed him and his way, though he did not will it so.

The Wandering Host

And he taught his companions, saying: *"We must seek his way in the nature of the things that abide. To learn this nature of things is the beginning of wisdom.*

For day unto day uttereth speech, and night unto night showeth knowledge.

The way of nature is solid, substantial, vast, and unchanging. He who walks in it stands secure, as in the shadow of a high tower or as if encompassed by a mighty fortress.

The wisdom of the forest shall be granted to him who seeks for it with calm heart and quiet eye."

But among his followers there were many who were eager and would hasten on, and although they spoke much of the Nature of Things and of the Law of the Forest, they were contented with speaking. *"The road is long,"* they said to themselves, *"and the hours are fleeting."*

They had no time to contemplate the glory of the heavens.

The beauty of the lilies fell on unobservant eyes.

For all these things they trusted to the report of others. The words passed from mouth to mouth, losing ever a little of their truth.

And in this, wise the voice of wisdom, was turned to the language of folly.

The Wandering Host

For the Nature of things is Truth.

Fourth Source Explorations

But no man can find truth except he seek it for himself.

The Wandering Host

And so they fared on, each well or ill, according to the truth to which his way bore witness.

Fourth Source Explorations

Meanwhile those who bore the white banner remained long in council.

At last one remembered that it was written, *"Faith without works is dead, being alone."* And it was written again, *"Those who follow me in spirit must follow me in spirit and in truth."*

The essence of truth lies not in thought or feeling, but must be expressed in deeds.

Right feelings follow right actions. Thus it was with him; thus will it be with us.

The Wandering Host

Then they went their way together, doing good to one another. And each called his neighbor "brother" and some bore cups of cold water, and some balm for healing; some carried oil and wine and pots of precious ointment. To whomsoever they met they gave help and comfort. The hungry they fed. The thirsty were given drink. He who had fallen by the wayside was lifted up and strengthened, and the blessing of cleanliness was brought to him who lay in filth and shame. The blessing of him that was ready to perish came upon them, and the heart of the widow sang for joy.

Fourth Source Explorations

But soon those who were filled with zeal for good works were gathered together in great bands, and each band wished to magnify its work. In every way, to all men who asked, help was given. They searched out the lame and the blind, and brought them, that they might be healed. Cup after cup of cold water was given to the little ones, even to those who might bring water for themselves. They cared for the wounded wayfarer long after his wounds were made whole. It was their joy to bathe his limbs in oil and wine, or to swathe them in fragrant bands. And the wayfarer ceased to bear his own tent or to seek his own raiment. What others would do for him, he need not do for himself. And those who did not help themselves lost the power of self-help. And those who had helped others overmuch came themselves to need the help of others.

The Wandering Host

At last the number of the helpless became so great that there was no one to serve them. Many waited day after day for the aid that never came, and they grew so weak with waiting that they could not take up their burdens. The little ones were thrust aside by the strong, and as the band went on many of them were forgotten and left behind. They fainted and fell by the healing springs, because there was no one to give them drink, and they could not help themselves.

And the burden of the way grew very hard and grievous to bear. Then there were those who said that one cannot help another save by leading him to help himself. All that is given him must he repay. Sooner or later each must bear his own burden. Each must make his own way through the forest in such manner as he may.

Fourth Source Explorations

So they turned back to the old Chart.

They would read his words again, that they might be led to better deeds. In these words they found help and cheer.

These words spake they one to another.

They came like rain to a thirsty field, or as balm to a wound, or as good news from a far country.

And there was wonderful consolation in the thought that for every step of the way he had spoken the right word.

The Wandering Host

So those who knew his words best were chosen as leaders, and great companies followed them.

And as band after band passed along, his message sounded from one to another. His words were ever on their lips.

Those who could run swiftly carried them far and wide, even into the depths of the forest. To those who were in sorrow they came as glad tidings of great joy, and beautiful upon the mountains seemed the feet of those who bore them. Wherever men were weary and heavy-laden, they were cheered by his promise of rest.

Fourth Source Explorations

But there were some who turned to his message only to gratify sordid hopes or vain desires. He who was lazy sought warrant for sleep. He who was covetous looked for gain. He who was filled with anger sought promise of vengeance. There were many who repeated his words for the mere words' sake. And there were some who used them in disputations about the way. And the words of help on the Chart they turned into words of command. Each one took these commands not to himself alone, but sought to enforce them upon others. *"For it is our duty,"* they said, *"to see that no word of his shall be unheeded of any man."*

And many rose in resistance. And the conflicts on the way were fierce and strong; for with each different band there was diversity of interpretation. Thus the words of kindness became the voice of hate.

The Wandering Host

And it came to pass that all along the way the green sward was red with the blood of wayfarers.

Everywhere the leaves of the forest were trampled by struggling hosts. And *"In his name,"* was the watch-word of each warring band. And each band called itself *"his army."* And whosoever bore the sword that was reddest, they called the *"Defender of the Faith."*

They placed his name upon their battle-flags, and beneath it they wrote these fearful words, *"In this sign conquer."* And each went forth to conquer his neighbor, and the wayfarer fled from the sight of their banners as from a pestilence.

Fourth Source Explorations

But *"Conquer, conquer,"* was no word of his.

He spoke not of victory over others; only of conquest of oneself.

He had said, *"Resist not, but overcome evil with good."*

And till all men ceased to resist and ceased to conquer, no one found himself in the right way.

Then some one said: *"By words alone can no one truly follow him. His words without his faith and love are like sounding brass or tinkling cymbal. Out of the abundance of the heart the mouth speaketh. When the heart is empty, the speech of the mouth is idle as the crackling of thorns beneath a pot."*

The Wandering Host

And there appeared other bands from the number of those who had passed to the right of the first great rock; and seeing the tumult and confusion of the others, they said to themselves: *"These are they who followed not us. We have chosen the better part. Our leader bears the only perfect Chart. All other charts are the invention of men. In the right Chart there can be nothing false; in the others there can be nothing true. Those who have not the true Chart can never go right, not even for a moment. For even good deeds done in the paths of evil must partake of the nature of sin. Straight is the way and narrow is the gate, but there is no safety except ye walk therein."*

Fourth Source Explorations

So they went on, stumbling ever along the rocky road, never resting, never murmuring. *"For the way at best is a vale of tears,"* said they, "and no one would have it otherwise. He found it thus in his time. He was ever a man of sorrows and acquainted with grief. More than all others had he suffered. It was his glory to be despised and rejected of men. For the greater the abasement, the greater the exaltation in the land beyond the river." So day by day they walked in the hardest part of the road. But they spoke often together of a land of pure delight, of sweet fields beyond the swelling floods, and of turf soft as velvet that rose from the river's bank.

The Wandering Host

If perchance on the way they came to green pastures, they would hasten on, lest they should be tempted to rest before the day of rest was come. From sweet springs they turned aside, that theirs might be the greater satisfaction when they came to the sweetest springs of all.

They shut their eyes to beauty and their ears to music, that the light and music of the unknown shore might burst upon them as a sudden revelation.

They looked not at the stars, lest perchance these should declare a glory which was reserved for the land beyond the river.

Dreary and harsh was the way they trod. But in its very dreariness they found safety.

They sought no pleasure, they fought no battles, they wasted no time. In the pushing aside of all temptation, the scorn of all beauty and idleness, they found delight.

Against the strength of granite rock they set the force of iron will. Withal, at the bottom their hearts were light with the certainty of coming joy.

Fourth Source Explorations

Even the multitude of conflicting paths gave them a peculiar satisfaction; for whatever way they took was always the right way.

But there were some among them who lost all heart. And they threw their charts away and set forth in disorder through the forest and up the mountain.

Some of them came safely to the river, far in advance of the bands they had left behind. But to most the way was strange, and harder than of old.

And as the journey wore on they began to hate the forest and all its ways.

The Wandering Host

So they fared on, together or apart, in ever-deepening shadow. They distrusted their neighbors. They despised the joyous bands who trooped after their leaders with mouthing of verses and waving of flags.

They were stirred by the sound of no trumpet. They were deceived by no illusion of sunshine or of mist.

They said: *"We know the forest; no one knows it but ourselves. There is no future; there is no way; there is no rest; there is no better country. The azure mists are shadows only, hiding some dreary plain, if haply they hide anything at all. Evil is man; evil are all things about him. Love and joy, hope and faith, all these are but flickering lights that lure him to destruction. Vultures croak on the rocks. The fountains flow with ink. Danger lurks in the desert. The name of the river is Death."*

And when they came to the shore of the river they saw no rift in the clouds above it, for their eyes were filled with gloom.

Fourth Source Explorations

But as time passed on, the way of man grew brighter, whether he would or no. No day or hour was without its joy to him who opened his heart to receive it. And men saw that most of the difficulties! and dangers of the way were those which they unwittingly had made for themselves or for others. Thus, as the road became more secure, it no longer seemed dreary or lonely.

The Wandering Host

And so it came to pass at last that men ceased to gather themselves in great bands. Nor did they longer set store on the sound of trumpets or the waving of flags. The men who were wisest ceased to be leaders of hosts. They became teachers and helpers instead.

And with all this a sure way was from day to day not hard to find. Men fell into it naturally and synchronistically. And the ways which are safe are innumerable as the multitude of those that may walk therein.

Fourth Source Explorations

"In my Father's house," so the Chart said, *"there are many mansions, and each mansion has its different setting, and diverse are the paths which lead to it."*

The Wandering Host

And those who had gone by devious ways came from time to time together. Each praised the charms of the path he had taken, but each one knew that in other paths other men found as great delight.

And as time went on many wise men passed over the way, and each in his own fashion left a record of all that had come to him.

Fourth Source Explorations

But the old Chart men kept in ever-increasing reverence. They found that its simple, honest words were words of truth, and whoso sought for truth gained with it courage and strength. But they covered it no longer with their own additions and interpretations.

The Wandering Host

Nor did any one insist that what he found helpful to himself should be law unto others.

No longer did men say to one another, *"This path have I taken; this way must thou go."*

And someone wrote upon the Chart this single rule of the forest: *"Choose thou thine own best way, and help thy neighbor to find that way which for him is best."*

But this was erased at last; for beneath it they found the older, plainer words which One in earlier times had written there,
>*"Thy neighbor as thyself."*

Fourth Source Explorations

*Men told me, Lord, it was a vale of tears
Where Thou hast placed me, wickedness and woe
My twain companions whereso I might go;
That I through ten and threescore weary years
Should stumble on beset by pains and fears,
Fierce conflict round me, passions hot within,
Enjoyment brief and fatal and din.
When all was ended then should I demand
Full compensation from thine austere hand;
For, 'tis thy pleasure, all temptation past,
To be not just but generous at last.*

*Lord, here am I, my threescore years and ten
All counted to the full; I've fought thy fight,
Crossed thy dark valleys, scaled thy rocks' harsh height,
Borne all the burdens Thou dost lay on men
With hand unsparing threescore years and ten.
Before Thee now I make my claim, O Lord,
What shall I pray Thee as a fair reward?
I ask for nothing. Let the balance fall!
All that I am or know or may confess
But swells the weight of mine indebtedness;
Burdens and sorrows stand transfigured all;
Thy hand's rude buffet turns to a caress,
For Love, with all the rest, Thou gavest me here,
And Love is Heaven's very atmosphere.
Lo, I have dwelt with Thee, Lord. Let me die.
I could no more through all eternity.*

MATRIKA PRESS SELECTIONS

Therese's Dream – Maine to Darfur: A Doctor's Story,
chronicles Dr. David Austin's time with Doctors Without Borders and illustrates the common humanity of peoples around the world. Dr. Austin is a lifelong Unitarian Universalist who has dedicated his life to healing and service.
http://MatrikaPress.com/dr-david-austin/

Where the Sky has No Stars
is a poetry anthology by Wesley Burton. His contemplative and imaginative poetry entices readers to face moments of transition. His words explore the inner depths of the psyche, the healing power of nature, and the soul's resilience to move forward out of darkness.
http://MatrikaPress.com/wesley-burton/

She Stood There
is a poem that has been read during blessingways and memorials, as well as for quiet contemplation and meditation. For three decades it has touched hearts and minds as individuals reflect on decisions made when life presents a crossroads, transition, choices and change. This is a single poem arranged in a pocket-size book (4x6). It is the first in our series: *A Pocketful book by Matrika Press.*
http://MatrikaPress.com/she-stood-there

A Pocketful book by Matrika Press can be a book of quotes, a meditation, a poem, or a series of thoughts brought forward for contemplation.

We are accepting submissions for pocket-size books, visit:

www.MatrikaPress.com

Seventh Principle Studies & First Source Explorations

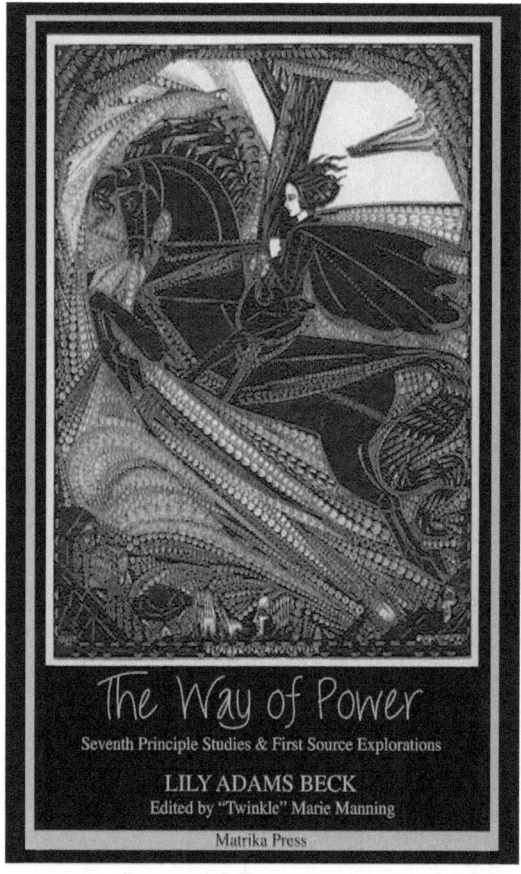

The 7th Unitarian Universalist Principle is: *"Respect for the interdependent web of all existence of which we are a part."* The first Source Unitarian Universalists draw faith from is: *"Direct experience of that transcending mystery and wonder, affirmed in all cultures, which moves us to a renewal of the spirit and an openness to the forces which create and uphold life."* Evidence to support such is found within the pages of ***The Way of Power***.

www.MatrikaPress.com

RECOMMENDED SELECTIONS FROM CHB MEDIA

CHB MEDIA POETRY ANTHOLOGIES —
Including the poetry of Twinkle Marie Manning

Poetry to Feed the Spirit
A Contemporary Anthology
of Central Florida Poets, Volume 1

Love & Other Passions
A Contemporary Anthology
of Central Florida Poets, Volume 2

Buy online at chbmediaonline.com, amazon.com, or barnesandnoble.com

RECOMMENDED SELECTIONS FROM BEACON PRESS

Claiming the Spirit Within
This wonderful book, edited by Rev. Marilyn Sewell, is a beautiful sourcebook of poetry and prose. A rich and diverse anthology dedicated to the praise of life, it presents the sacredness that emerges when women immerse fully in living lives of spirit while embracing the physical. Its contents include more than 300 poems celebrating all aspects of women's lives. Contributors include Margaret Atwood, Rita Dove, Louise Erdrich, Tess Gallagher, Nikki Giovanni, Joy Harjo, and Maxine Hong Kingston.

A Chosen Faith: *An Introduction to Unitarian Universalism*
Authored by Forrest Church and John A. Buehrens, this book offers a an informative look at Unitarian Universalism. The authors explore the history and sources of this living tradition. For those contemplating religious choices, Unitarian Universalism offers an appealing alternative to religious denominations that stress theological creeds over individual conviction and belief. It allows room for individual interpretations of the sacred and encourages affirming diversity, personal choice, shared experiences, rites of passage, religious education and work for social justice.

http://www.beacon.org/

Should you wish to Publish your work, visit our website for submission guidelines. Please note: As an independent publisher, we *do* accept unsolicited manuscripts at this time.

www.MatrikaPress.com

AVAILABLE NOW FROM MATRIKA PRESS

www.MatrikaPress.com

RECOMMENDED SELECTIONS FROM SKINNER HOUSE

Finding the Voice Inside: *Writing As a Spiritual Quest for Women*

Gail Collins-Ranadive offers forty practical and imaginative writing exercises that invite women to explore their uniquely feminine spirituality. Through writing of symbols, metaphors and truths of their own lives, women re-awaken to higher truths of their sacredness.

Reaching for the Sun

Rev. Angela Herrera's book of meditations, prayers and invocations provide inspiration to readers and serve as a resource to those seeking powerful liturgical words, grounded in the experiences of everyday life.

Evening Tide

This book of mediations by Elizabeth Tarbox helps readers to face the darker moments of life, the challenging circumstances that call us to live more fully even when we feel our most empty.

http://www.uua.org/publications/skinnerhouse

ISBN: 978-1-946088-02-4

www.ingramcontent.com/pod-product-compliance
Lightning Source LLC
Chambersburg PA
CBHW021157080526
44588CB00008B/389